Whispers In The Dark

Jheel Shah

BookLeaf Publishing

India | USA | UK

Copyright © Jheel Shah
All Rights Reserved.

This book has been self-published with all reasonable efforts taken to make the material error-free by the author. No part of this book shall be used, reproduced in any manner whatsoever without written permission from the author, except in the case of brief quotations embodied in critical articles and reviews.

The Author of this book is solely responsible and liable for its content including but not limited to the views, representations, descriptions, statements, information, opinions, and references ["Content"]. The Content of this book shall not constitute or be construed or deemed to reflect the opinion or expression of the Publisher or Editor. Neither the Publisher nor Editor endorse or approve the Content of this book or guarantee the reliability, accuracy, or completeness of the Content published herein and do not make any representations or warranties of any kind, express or implied, including but not limited to the implied warranties of merchantability, fitness for a particular purpose.

The Publisher and Editor shall not be liable whatsoever...

Made with ❤ on the BookLeaf Publishing Platform
www.bookleafpub.in
www.bookleafpub.com

Dedication

*To anyone who has ever sought for solace in the dark
and sat with their hammering thoughts—
These whispers are for you.*

Preface

"I whisper in the dark,
Hoping you feel heard too.
A silent prayer in the thick air,
Hoping you'll find your way too."

Whispers in the Dark is a collection born from the quiet places within us—a fragment drawn from experiences of love, loss, healing, longing, and hope. Each poem in this collection is a whisper reaching out to you—an invitation to feel, to reflect, and perhaps to find comfort in knowing you are not alone. May these pages of hushed but vulnerable, raw, and honest confessions meet you gently, wherever you are.

Acknowledgements

This collection would not exist without the support and inspiration of many.

To my family and friends, thank you for listening to my whispers in the dark and being my guiding light.

To the people in my life who encourage me to be a better person, and provide me with daily motivation through their words and actions, thank you for never leaving my side.

To myself, for believing in the power of the words I write.

To the readers, thank you for opening these pages and hearing the whispers. May they find you like a lantern in the dark.

The Masks I Wear

I've crafted masks with careful hands,
One for my family—strong, composed,
One for my friends—lighthearted, free,
Each one perfect, flawlessly posed.

They see me smile, they hear me laugh,
A version tailored to their view,
But in the dark, when no one's watching,
The truest self begins to bloom.

No polished words, no careful grace,
Just raw reflections in the night,
A whispered voice, a weary face,
A soul unmasked, devoid of light.

Yet even there, beneath the weight,
Of roles I play and truths I hide,
I wonder—if I stripped them all,
Would I still know who lives inside?

Hope

Hope,
Can you see it with your naked eyes,
Like the sun peeking through weary skies?
Or does it whisper in the dark,
A silent spark, a beating heart?

Hope,
Can you feel it with your eyes closed,
Like a warmth where the cold wind blows?
A gentle hand upon your chest,
A promise made, a soul caressed?

Hope,
Can you touch it with your bare hands,
Like grains of time slipping through sands?
Or does it linger in your grip,
A fragile dream, a steadfast ship?

Hope,
Do you understand it well enough

To pass it on when times are tough?
A spark to share, a flame to grow,
A gift to those who need it most.

Hope,
Do you believe in it, despite the pain,
Through trials harsh and skies of rain?
To reach beyond the darkest night,
And hold on tight to life's faint light?

The Weight of Me

Looking back, all I see
are tears—
mine, staining the past,
yours, falling because of me.

Darkness lingers where I stood,
not just a shadow,
but a storm I summoned,
pulling you in,
drowning you with me.

You say love's worth the struggle,
but I fear I'm a chain,
the links forged in our battles,
binding you to my pain.

You say you're proud,
you call me your favorite,
you promise you'd always choose me.
But I know, I really know—

I am not a choice,
I am a weight,
a burden you feel bound to bear.

And yet, you stay.
Even when the weight is me.

House of Shadows

i live in a house
with many walls,
no windows, and
a door locked
from inside.
it is suffocating in here,
and i know that
i might die
if i don't leave
this place or
knock the walls down
or break the door.

it's dark in here,
no light, no oxygen.
i feel like an almost dead,
with no hope of living.
strangely, (or not?)
but it's like
i have become

comfortable with
this environment,
like i have become
comfortable being
almost dead.

The Idea of Love

You will probably judge me
by the time you reach the end,
for the things I've done,
for the person I am beneath the skin.

They say love is easy,
and I won't disagree,
for I have fallen a thousand times—
in passing moments, in fleeting dreams.

With the stranger on the train
who met my gaze and held it still,
perhaps out of knowing,
or maybe just out of boredom.

With the man who spoke kindly,
his voice laced with warmth,
not love, not longing,
but something close enough.

I have loved in seconds,
in stolen glances and soft hellos,
in gestures too small to keep
but too deep to forget.

And maybe that's my curse—
to fall for the feeling,
for the idea of love itself,
never meant to stay, always meant to fade.

I Am Fine

when you ask me
how am i today,
i want to scream
that i am exhausted,
and want to be free.

i am tired of pretending,
that i am fine,
that it doesn't kill me;
the deafening noises—
both, from outside and inside.

i am tired of trying,
to smile more often,
to hope for better,
to love and live freely.
i am tired of trying today.

but i won't tell you this,
instead i put on a smile

which you won't notice is fake,
like many other things
and many other people.

and i'll tell you i am fine today.

Reflections in My Eyes

you say, you see many things in my eyes—
the dreams i wish to come true and
the broken dreams i once wished to come true,
the love that is sacred and
the love that has been scarred,
the hope of a better tomorrow and
the fear of a frightful past,
the joy that shines brightly like sun and
the tears that fall only in the dark,
the strength to fight alone and
the pain caused by people i once called my own,
the confidence like a flame flickering high and
the insecurities creeping like shadows behind,
the harsh realities and all the lies,
the best and the worst,
—for they are like the windows to my soul.

you say, you see love in my eyes
on the days i hesitate or struggle to say so, and that they
speak louder

than those commonly used words
uttered by some artifice mouths.
you say, you wish i didn't hate my brown eyes,
that i would meet them in the mirror,
not just in the eyes of another,
and finally see the beauty in their depth.
and then you say, you wish
i said those words to myself, too,
and loved myself enough
to not search it in the eyes of others.
you say, i leave you speechless,
and make you wonder if you're seeing yourself in me—
or if we are simply the same,
reflections caught in each other's eyes.

Your Whatever

Dear . . .

What are we?
Strangers passing in borrowed time,
friends tangled in quiet understanding,
or something more, unnamed, undefined?

You know me—too much, too well,
enough that I fear unraveling further,
enough that I wonder if one day,
you'll see the cracks and turn away.

You have traced the scars I hide,
held the parts I swore to bury,
and somehow, you stayed—
as if I were still something whole.

You feel unreal, like a dream I fear waking from,
like a truth too kind to belong to me.
But here we are, no masks, no walls,

only ourselves in each other's light.

What are we? I may never know.
But if we are nothing else,
we are this—
and that is enough.

Your whatever,
J.

Dawn and Midnight

it's sad, you know
that we are so different,
almost opposite of each other;
you're like the dawn,
the beginning of light
and i, just like the midnight,
too dark and too gloomy.

but it's sadder, you know
every time you come closer
and try to light me up
with your brilliancy,
i just do a fade
i don't know why.
or, maybe it's vice versa.

See You Again

My hands tremble,
Clutching the news I feared the most.
My lips quiver,
A knot tightens in my stomach,
My chest heavy with unspoken words.

You are leaving soon, the letter whispers.
Though I had seen this moment before,
Played it over in my restless mind,
It still steals my breath away.

I sit in silence,
Trying to think,
But my mind is too full of emptiness—
Too loud with nothing at all.

The shower runs,
Cold water rushes over me,
Yet it cannot wash away the void.
I flinch, touch my cheek,

No tears—
Not yet.

Now, the bus hums beneath me,
My head is suddenly alive,
A storm of thoughts,
A thousand questions with no answers.
The overthinker in me wakes,
Spinning futures I cannot see,
Imagining endings I do not want.

Then, it hits me.

Maybe I will never see you again.
Maybe this is the last goodbye.
Maybe when you return,
I will be gone—
Not moved on,
But moved beyond,
To a place with no return.

And finally, the tears come.

Slow at first, then faster,
Falling, slipping, streaming,
Leaving silent scars upon my skin.

But then—
A thought.

A whisper from somewhere deep,
A flicker of light in the dark.
I want to live.
Live enough to see you again,
To hear your voice,
To feel the warmth of your words once more.

I press a hand to my chest,
A quiet promise to myself.
I will wait.
I will stay.
I will live—
And I will see you again.

A Mother's Words

"You look beautiful when you keep your hair that way,"
my mother says, watching me comb through the tangles,
for once, not minding the strands falling in my lap like
autumn leaves.

"For that, I guess I need a beautiful face too,"
I joke, with a half-formed smile,
glancing at her, searching for a shift, a sign.
But her expression stays the same, steady, certain.

"Come on, you're beautiful.
You don't see yourself the way you should.
Look at yourself through a boy's eyes."
She smiles, waiting, watching—
does she expect me to blush?

"Well, no boy has ever said so,"
I reply, forcing a smile that doesn't quite fit.
She pauses, lips pressed in thought,
a look I cannot decipher, a silence too heavy to hold.

"Maybe the fault is in their eyes.
Maybe the fault is with the boys,"
she says, adjusting her glasses,
and I let out a chuckle, light but trembling.
We laugh, and laugh,
until the laughter turns quiet,
until my eyes are wet,
and I do not know why.

"You're absolutely beautiful," she tells me,
her voice full of something I cannot name.
I want to ask if she means it,
or if love has made her blind to the truth—
but I don't.

Instead, I sit there,
letting her words wrap around me,
like a warmth I am still learning to believe in.

Goodbyes

Dear You,

I don't know if you're reading this,
if my words will ever reach you,
but the questions remain,
echoing in the silence you left behind.

Tell me—
what will you do with our memories?
Will you lock them away,
or let them fade like dust in the wind?

What about my secrets,
the truths I whispered in the dark?
Will you keep them safe,
or scatter them like fallen leaves?

Will I become just another name,
another fool in your story?
Will you call me what you called the rest—

a dumb bitch for daring to think differently?

I wonder, but I may never know.
And maybe that's the real goodbye—
not in the leaving,
but in the questions left unanswered.

Tiny Little Love

do you remember the nights
we'd spend on the rooftops
of the houses long abandoned,
where only the wind could hear us,
as we whispered our lies?

do you remember the nights
we'd spend on the dark-dark streets
people didn't choose to walk,
where shadows wrapped around us
like a secret never meant to be seen?

do you remember the nights
we'd spend together,
to hide our tiny little secret,
to hide ourselves,
to hide our tiny little love?

Music

On my hardest days,
when the world feels too heavy,
I could scream into the abyss
and still—somehow—you would hear me.

You and your music,
a melody wrapped around my sorrow,
a rhythm that holds me steady
when everything else falls apart.

You don't need to answer,
don't need to speak—
just being there is enough,
just listening is enough.

So I close my eyes,
let the sound carry my pain,
knowing that no matter how far I fall,
you and your music will catch me again.

Colourblind

my mother used to say,
that people change colours
just like the evening sky,
that they are unpredictable
and you'd never know
the next colour,
that every colour you find beautiful
is just going to turn into black with time.

i never really thought
or cared about her, her words,
for they were too deep
to my naive, innocent mind.
i wish i believed her earlier,
or didn't laugh at her words then,
or just didn't become colourblind
after meeting you.

From Afar

I have seen you,
but only from far, far away.
A whisper of light in the evening glow,
a dream that never fades.

You look beautiful—
like dawn spilling gold on quiet streets,
like the hush of moonlight on restless seas,
amazing and inspiring,
a spark that turns the dark to peace.

Sometimes childish,
laughing like raindrops on eager leaves.
Sometimes mature,
a silent strength the wind believes.
Sometimes flirtatious,
a glance that lingers, a teasing breeze.
Sometimes gentle,
soft as petals in the springtime ease.

I have seen you,
but only from far, far away.
Perhaps one day, I'll reach you,
no longer worlds apart.
But even if I never do,
I know you will shine within my heart.

Sun and Pluto

you are the sun—
radiant, blinding and untouchable.
you are the cynosure of all eyes,
drawing people to your golden glow,
making them orbit around you.

i am pluto—
distant, cold, and forgotten.
drifting on the edge of existence,
too small to matter,
too far to be seen.

you burn with brilliance,
while i linger in shadow,
always watching, never reaching,
knowing i will never be
part of your orbit.

Shadow

she fell in love with her shadow,
for it didn't bear her scars,
the dark blue bruises under her eyes.

she fell in love with her shadow,
for it didn't have a face,
and it made her feel beautiful.

she fell in love with her shadow,
for it never questioned her,
or made her pretend to be fine.

she fell in love with her shadow,
for it was a ghost of her deepest hopes,
always there, even when she felt alone.

she fell in love with her shadow,
for it never judged the mess inside,
only mirrored the love she couldn't see.

she fell in love with her shadow,
for it promised a love that would linger,
even when daybreak chased it away.

And So I Wait

*"You are supposed to wait
endlessly for the people you love."*
And so I wait—

Till the sun melts into the horizon,
painting the sky in a fading fire.
Till the moon hums in silver silence,
whispering secrets to the tides.

Till the wind turns cold and cruel,
stealing warmth from my trembling hands.
Till the leaves turn gold, then bare,
scattering memories across the earth.

Till the echoes of laughter grow faint,
lost in the chambers of time.
Till my shadow grows smaller,
swallowed by the weight of years.

And still, I wait—

through shifting seasons, through endless nights,
because it is you
I am waiting for.

Daughters of Fire

They told us to whisper and lower our gaze,
To walk in the shadows, to quiet our blaze.
To hold our breaths and unclench our teeth,
To shrink ourselves and hide underneath.

They told us to fold our wings, stay small,
To minimise our vision, to never stand tall.
But fire runs fierce through the veins of the bold,
A story of women both young and old.

Built up by dreams broken and scattered,
By screams unheard, by voices shattered.
We are the daughters of those silenced before,
Echoes of strength that will rise evermore.

No longer afraid, no longer confined,
We carry the battles of those left behind.
With fire in our voices, with light in our eyes,
We shatter the chains—they fall as we rise.

Fragments of Me

I hold the fragments of my heart in my hands,
The sharp edges press deep into my skin,
Each shard a memory, each crack a story,
Waiting for someone to piece me together again.

I hold them close, though they cut and bleed,
Hoping someone will see the brokenness I hide,
To heal the jagged parts of me,
And place them where they once resided, side by side.

But the pieces tremble, fragile, worn,
And I wonder if they'll ever fit the same,
If they'll ever be whole again,
Or if I'm meant to carry their weight in silence, and in
pain.

So I wait in the stillness, hoping,
For a touch, a word, a sign—
To make me whole again,
And find a place where my heart feels safe.

Red

red,
is the colour of whispers in the dark,
secrets painted in hushed tones,
binding the fragile threads of trust.

red,
is the colour of danger—
of hatred, of threat—
camouflaged in the sweet disguise of love.

red,
is the colour of sunsets that bleed
into the horizon as day retreats,
a reminder that endings can be beautiful too.

red,
is the colour of my body's grief,
a monthly bloom of silent cries,
a storm that wilts me from within.

red,
is the colour of my heart, bare and brave,
offered up to every kind hand,
too eager to believe in warmth.

red,
is the colour of anger that simmers,
a fire ignited by injustice,
fueling the fight for what is right.

red,
is the colour of the curtain at the end of the play,
drawn slowly, dramatically—
a bow to all that was felt but never said.

Whispers in the Dark

i sit in the silence under the moonlight,
and whisper into the nothingness,
hoping my voice gets heard somewhere,
a distant echo to someone's ear.

a sea of thoughts surround me,
an ocean of unresolved questions,
a pool where my feet touch the bottom,
and yet i choose to drown.

this is a never-ending cycle,
one that i decide to pedal myself,
and lose control as soon as
the path takes a new turn.

is there ever an end to this?
this unrelenting train of thoughts,
the worries of the world,
the overwhelming darkness that lingers?

www.ingramcontent.com/pod-product-compliance
Lightning Source LLC
LaVergne TN
LVHW051238200726

843510LV00011B/1602